Quiet thoughts, loud words.

Rachelle Bekker

Presentation by *BookLeaf Publishing*

Web: www.bookleafpub.com

E-mail: info@bookleafpub.com

ISBN: 9789357446464

First edition 2022

DEDICATION

To my little bird,

Without you I could not have done this.

I am very grateful that you keep pushing to bring out the best in me.

Thank you.

Love, me

PREFACE

When people think of poetry and poems most of them think of poems that rhyme. Poems however do not have to rhyme at all. I personally enjoy writing free verse poems. My poems almost never rhyme, but that doesn't make them any worse or better than other poems.

Life as I know it

Life as I know it may differ from what you know. What I know to be true might not be truthful at all. My experiences may differ from yours, yet we are both here, together.

The same but different.
Equal and yet not.

The exact same circumstances can shape two people in mesmerizingly different ways.

Unique and still identical.

Lotus flower

Lotus flowers can grow in the muddiest of waters. To some the lotus flower is a spiritual symbol of growth. Growth can happen even in the darkest of places. Just like a lotus flower. When a lotus flower is growing it is not yet clear what colour it will be. Just like with us. When we are growing it is not yet clear who we will be. Even though you may not know what colour you will become, you are growing every single day.

The colour of a lotus flower can vary from flower to flower, just like with us. Some yellow like the sun, some a beautiful shade of blue. Once your true colour finally shows you can look back with pride and say that you made it.

I would say every colour is beautiful, just like with us. Unfortunately not everyone agrees yet.

Home

The feeling of home, what is that?
Some say it is the feeling of a big tight hug.
Some say it is the feeling of being free to be yourself. Some say it is being able to lay on the couch all day with no shame. Some say home is where the heart is.

To me the feeling of home means to feel safe and loved. Not everyone is so lucky to have grown up in a safe or a loved home. Sometimes the very people who are supposed to love you most do not make you feel safe at all. Some people do not even have a place to call home at all.

What makes you feel like home?

A letter to me

Dear younger me,

There will be hard moments in life. Moments where you might even want to give up. You will look up at the sky someday in despair yelling out that life is not fair. Younger than me you may be but the truth spoken from your mouth like an old soul.

Life is not fair.

Some people never had to worry about money a day in their lives. To some people that's all they can think about.Some people can eat pizza and ice cream for breakfast and be totally fine. Some people only have to look at a donut a certain way to gain weight.Some people are born as girls or boys or anything in between or even both.Some people are born black, or white.

There are unfair differences all around us. Treating people differently because of that is what is unfair to me.

1921

If you look back 100 years ago, Times were so different then. Just a few years after the first World War, although back then it wasn't the first it was the only. If only we could tell people that a second World War was coming. Would that change anything?

Do you think that our ancestors could have imagined the lives we get to live today? Mobile phones and the internet are almost if not completely in control of everyday life. How different our lives have become but also how the same it has stayed.

People are still poor.

People still discriminate.

Yet we don't have flying cars. How did that happen?

quation of time

As a kid you have all the time in the world. The summer Holliday seems like an endless sea of time. You also have enough energy to do everything you want to do. The only thing you do not have is money.

As you reach adulthood and start earning more money, you still have enough energy, but you start to lose the time to do the things you love.

When you retire you have more money and you once again have all the time in the world, although everyone around you seems too busy. Maybe that is a good thing though because you seem to lose the energy to do things.

Every phase in life has its complexities.

Prioritize.

A books cover

Whether you like it or not you are judged by others every time someone sees you. Every time you say a word. Every time you do anything at all. Someone somewhere will judge you. An opinion is formed within 0,1 seconds. You do that too. I do too. It's natural human behaviour to do so. There is nothing you can do about it happening.

But you can be aware.

If you are aware of this behaviour you might take an extra 0,2 seconds to think of something nicer. Maybe that fat lady in the supermarket whom you thought should just loose some weight is desperately trying. Maybe that college who goes home early every day is not unwilling, he just needs to pick up his child. Maybe that homeless person is not spending the money you gave him on drugs or alcohol, but using it to buy food for his dog.

Never judge a book by its cover.

Greener grass

You can have the most beautiful garden filled with flowers and trees. You can literally wake up to the sight of deers and squirrels playing in your pond and still look over to your neighbour who's grass is greener and more beautiful than yours. You'll forget the fact that your grass is missing small patches because deer feel safe enough to graze. You'll forget that you have beautiful flowers that attract stunningly coloured butterflies and that your neighbour has fake flowers because those are less trouble. You'll forget that you have trees that grow delicious fruits and houses a family of squirrels, while your neigbour just cut down his tree because he was sick of cleaning up the leaves.

The grass is greener on the other side.

His grass may be greener but do not lose sight of what you have.

Time flies

"Time is going by so much faster than I"

We all know the saying 'time flies when you are having fun. Well in my opinion time also flies in daily life. Where you are not having fun per se, but just live your life. It flies by.

It is September now and it feels like the summer holiday just started a week or 2 ago.

It feels like just last week that my little sister was 12 years old. Well in reality, she is 20 now. Seriously, how did that happen?It also feels like yesterday that I talked to my grandpa, while it has been 2 weeks already.

In day to day life you start to forget things, you are busy and just do not have much time.People grow up right before your eyes. All you have to do is blink once or twice.

At the same time people also grow old. Weeks go by, months go by, years go by. Suddenly you are out of time.

Make time.

All lives matter

Black white , brown or blue.

If only we could choose the colour of our skin. Would that help? Or would it just make it worse? Would we find some other non important reason to exclude and ridicule someone.

Too bad we can't choose the colour of our skin anymore than you could choose the size your feet grow to be.

You might laugh and think to yourself why on earth you would shame someone for the size of their feet, that is just ridiculous. You can not do anything about the size of your feet.

Exactly.

Magnificent tree

Trees can easily grow to be a few thousand years old. If we leave them alone that is.

Trees spread their roots as far as 5 times the canopy radius. Which means it will grow roots as far out as it needs to flourish, but not too far so the roots thin out. If there are multiple bigger trees in the same area, the roots will go around each other so every tree can spread their roots equally.

Trees are also stronger together. If there would be only one tree with one set of roots we could easily extract that tree. If there are two, three or more trees, they will hold onto each other. Roots underneath and on top of other roots. That makes it way harder to even extract a single tree.

Maybe we are kind of like trees.

Stronger together.

If only we would let other people have the space to spread out their roots too.

Past life

Everyone has one. A past. Some good. Some bad. Once it has gone by it will never come back. You can only look at it from afar. Further and further away each passing day. Your life keeps going, it does not stop, it does not take breaks, but you are not really there.

The further and longer you go back in time to visit the past the more you miss of this life now. At this time. This too will be past.

Just like this poem. Once you read it, it can not be undone. You can go back and reread it, but it will not be the same.

You can not change anything.

The past is the past.

What about now?

To let go

People hold on for a variation of possible
reasons. Comfort, fear or love. Different reasons
to achieve the same thing. To hold on.
Letting go means uncertainties. Uncertainties
could also mean something bad. Or something
good. However the fear of the unknown is quite
strong.Sometimes holding on is worse than
letting go.

How do you know when that moment is near?

I imagine it to be like a string. You are holding
on to one end, someone else is holding the other
end. You can twist the string, knot it, get lost in
it. However when both of you start pulling away
from each other, the string stretches a little, but it
can not keep stretching forever. Eventually it
will break and you will get hurt.

Will it not hurt when you let go sooner?

It might.

Only you can decide what is better for you.
As long as you remember that there is an option
to let go.

Small joys

In life you often worry about big things or you might get lost in day to day life. You get so busy you stop noticing the little things in life.

The smell of freshly cut grass for example.

Or the sunrise in the background as you drive to work.

The happiness it brings to see your goofy cat play.

The joy of someone really enjoying the meal you made them.

How grateful you feel it you are really tired and your partner cooks and cleans for you.

When you have to get up really early and hear all the birds chirping.

Getting a real compliment.

Do not lose track of these small moments of happiness.

These are mine, what are yours?

Step by step

You are defined by the things that you have done. Good or bad. The mistakes that you made.

Where you are now. Not how you got there. Even though getting here at all took tremendous amounts of effort.

I think learning is like walking stairs. You go up step by step. Sometimes the steps are easy and you can take 2 at a time. Sometimes you have to take a break and you sit on your step. Sometimes you fall a few steps and then you have to take those same steps again.

Would it not be great if you would be defined by how many steps it took you to get there instead of the actual achievement itself? That the more steps you had to take the harder you worked to achieve something?

Some things come easy, some things you really have to work for. What matters most is that you try.

Keep trying.
One step at a time.

Once in a blue moon

Life happens. It happens to everyone. Whether you like it or not. The good and the bad. Life is merciless. It never gives breaks, it never stops until it does.

Just because you can never catch a break does not mean you cannot recharge every once in a while.

Once every so often something so rare happens you have to cherish it. Moments that happen scarcely. Moments like falling in love, graduating, getting married or getting children I imagine.

Those moments that happen few and far between need to be held dear.Cherish those moments.

Maybe even use them to recharge.

But most importantly enjoy them as much as you possibly can. It might only happen once in a blue moon.

Up to you

You decide. This is your life and you make the decisions. People can have a certain influence, but you have to live with it.

Is this how you want to live your life?

Decide.

Does this make you happy?

Decide.

This life and the decisions that come with it are up to you. There is no point to keep doubting. If you want something different, decide.

It is all up to you.

To the moon and back

I will love you until the day I take my last breath. And if there is a way for me to continue loving you after that, I will do so.

Love is not easy. A relationship is even harder. You have to work for it every single day.

People make mistakes. I do, you do, we all do. Pick yourself up and dust yourself off and learn from it.

The journey to the moon and back is not exactly safe and easy either so I think the saying fits perfectly.

When you stand on top of the moon though, you will forget the hard path it took for you to get there. The view will be worth it.

Just like you.

You are my view.

You are worth it.

Till death do us part.

Nobody really knows what happens when we die. There are all kinds of different beliefs.

Heaven
Hell
Reincarnation
Ghosts
The immortal soul

There are no theories of what happens after you die, only hopes and dreams. I choose to believe that wherever I end up, it will be okay.

What has been proven is that we only have a limited time to be alive. Every living thing dies. Some way sooner than they should have and some are luckier. That is the balance of life.

Everyone dies. Also your loved ones.

Make sure that the people you love know that you love them.

Hold that hug just a little while longer.

You never know when it will be the last.

Love yourself

Almost every person is loved by many. Your parents, your siblings, your friends, your partner.

Some people have so many people that love them that they almost drown in it. Some people are lucky to find 1 person.

No matter how many or how few people love you, they do not have to be with you for 24 hours of 7 days a week.

You do.

They do not have to live with the choices you made.

You do.

They can step away if they wish to do so.

You cannot.

Nobody can love you like you can.

Learn to love yourself.

Goodbyes

Nobody wants to say goodbye. We avoid it at all costs. Yet there are so many goodbyes in our lives, many different ones as well.

Goodbye, see you soon.

Goodbye as the end of a conversation.

Goodbye as I will miss you.

Or the worst of all the goodbyes, the final goodbye.

Some people find it so hard they do not dare to say it at all. Some people can not say it enough.

Goodbyes are hard no matter how you say it.

Whether you say it a 100 times to make sure you did not miss that final time. Or you do not say it at all afraid that it will come true.

Goodbyes happen to all of us. Whether you say it or not. It still happens.

We must all say goodbye in the end.
Goodbye.